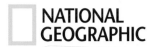

NATIONAL
GEOGRAPHIC

D0503640

I Can Breathe Underwater

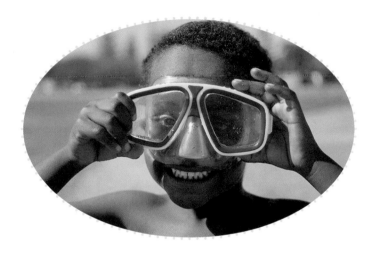

Pat Malone

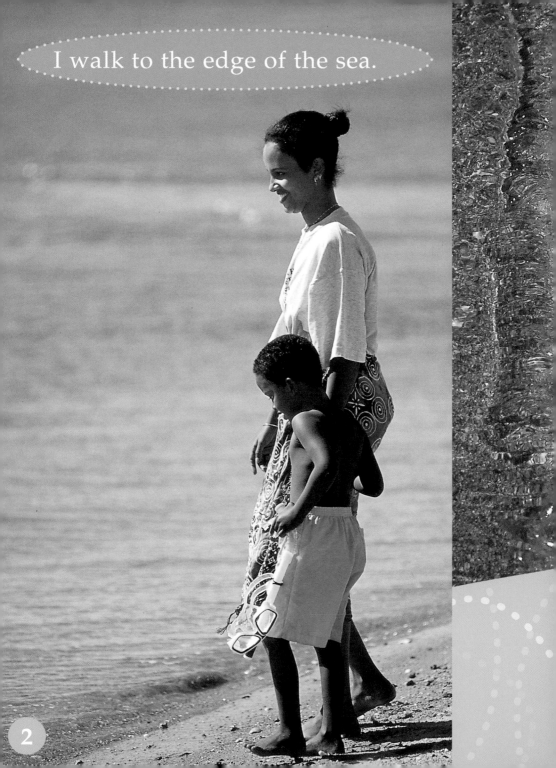

I walk to the edge of the sea.

2

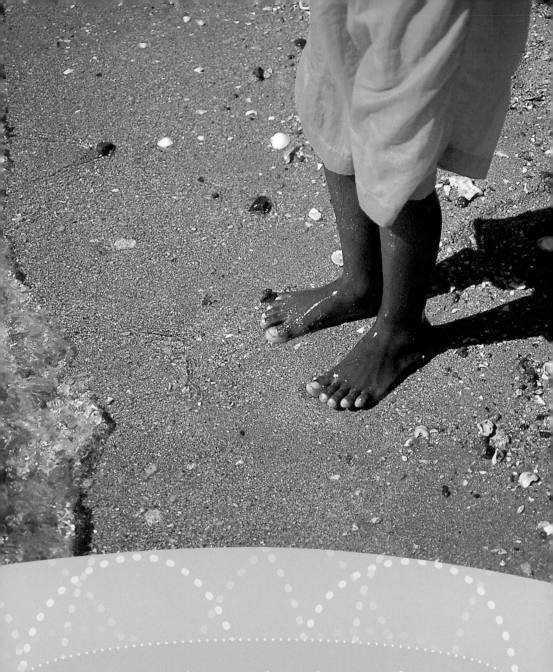

The sand is cool under my feet.

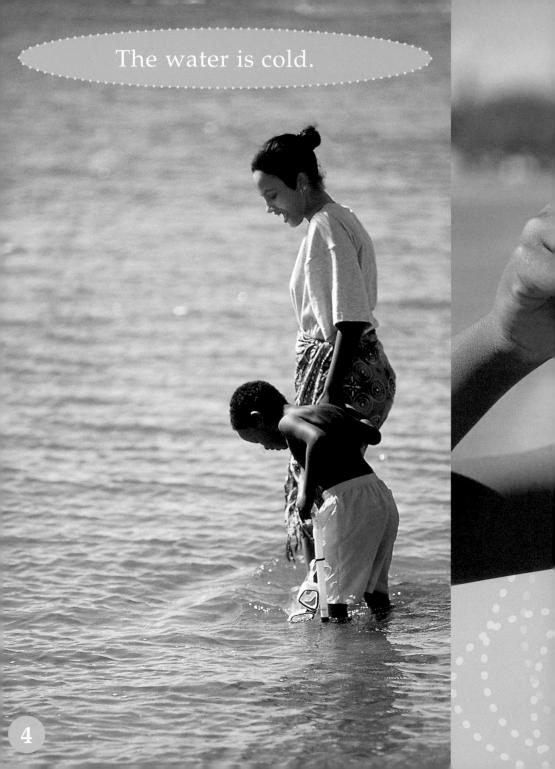

The water is cold.

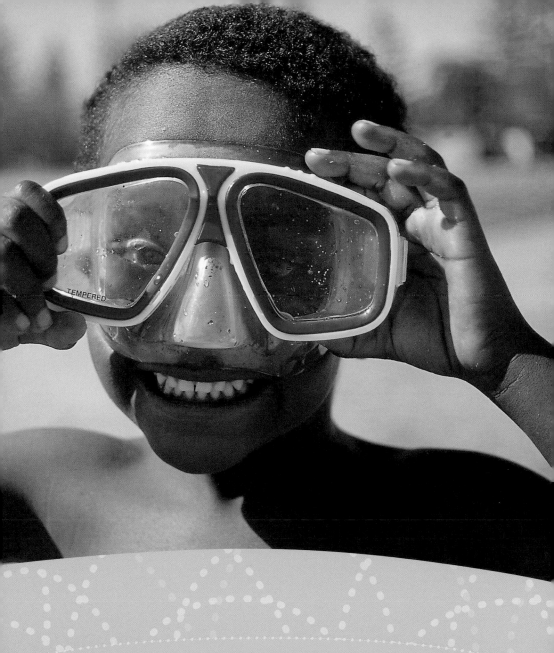

I put on my mask.

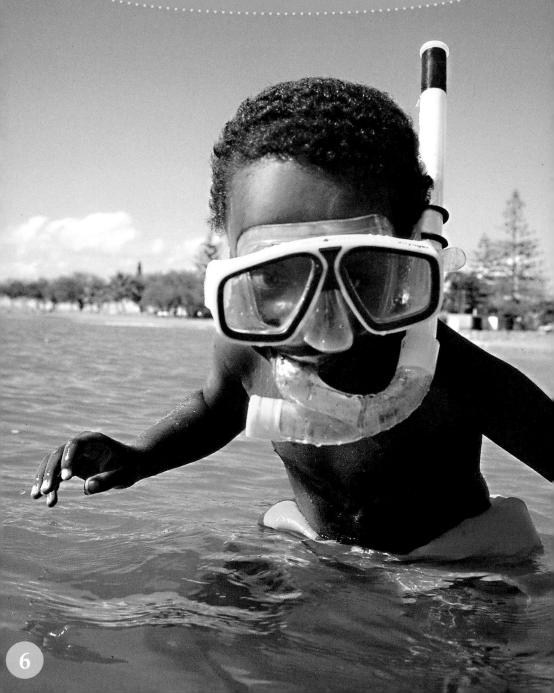

I put the snorkel in my mouth.

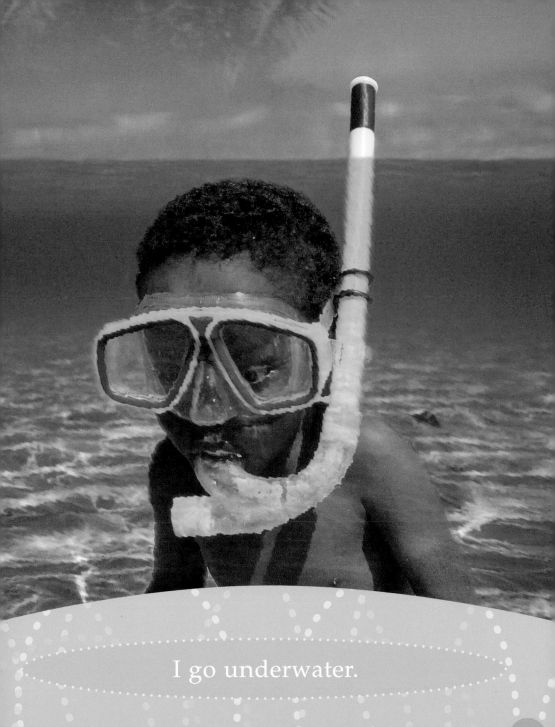

I go underwater.

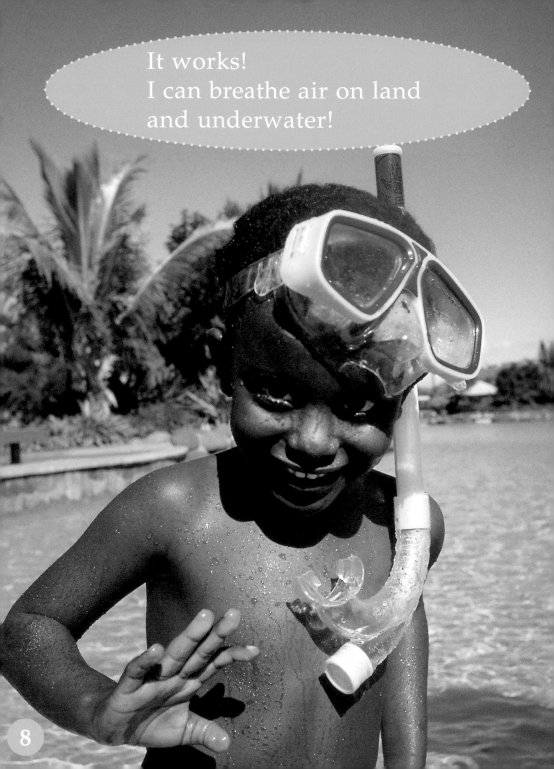